What Lives on a Prairie?

Janey Levy

Rosen Classroom Books & Materials
New York

Rosen
REAL READERS

Published in 2003 by The Rosen Publishing Group, Inc.
29 East 21st Street, New York, NY 10010

Book Design: Haley Wilson

Photo Credits: Cover, p. 1 © Richard Day/Animals Animals; cover, p. 15 (jackrabbit) © Johnathan Blair/Corbis; cover, p. 18 (great plains toad) © E. R. Degginger/Animals Animals; pp. 4–5, 10–11, 14–15, 16–17 (all), 18–19 , 20–21 © SuperStock; pp. 6–7 © Tom Bean/Corbis; pp. 6–7 (flower) © Pat O'Hara/Corbis; pp. 8–9 © Gallo Images/Corbis; p. 8 (inset) © Mike Zens/Corbis; p. 11 (white buffalo) © Joseph Sohm; ChromoSohm Inc./Corbis; pp. 12–13 © Margot Conte/Animals Animals; p. 15 (ferret) © D. Robert & Lorri Franz/Corbis; pp. 18–19 (skink & hognose snake) © Zig Leszczynski/Animals Animals; p. 19 (American toad) © Robert Lubeck/ Animals Animals.

ISBN: 0-8239-6390-X
6-pack ISBN: 0-8239-9575-5

Manufactured in the United States of America

CPSIA Compliance Information: Batch #WR412180RC:
For Further Information contact Rosen Publishing, New York, New York at 1-800-237-9932

Contents

What Is a Prairie?

A prairie is an area of flat or hilly land covered mostly by grasses and flowering plants. The middle of **North America** has three types of prairie. The tallgrass prairie is in the east and gets the most rain. The shortgrass prairie is in the west and gets little rain. In between is mixed-grass prairie. Summer **temperatures** on the prairie may rise above 100 degrees **Fahrenheit**. Winter temperatures may drop to 40 degrees below zero!

"Prairie" is a French word that means "meadow." Settlers called the prairie a "sea of grass" because the grasses waving in the wind reminded them of ocean waves.

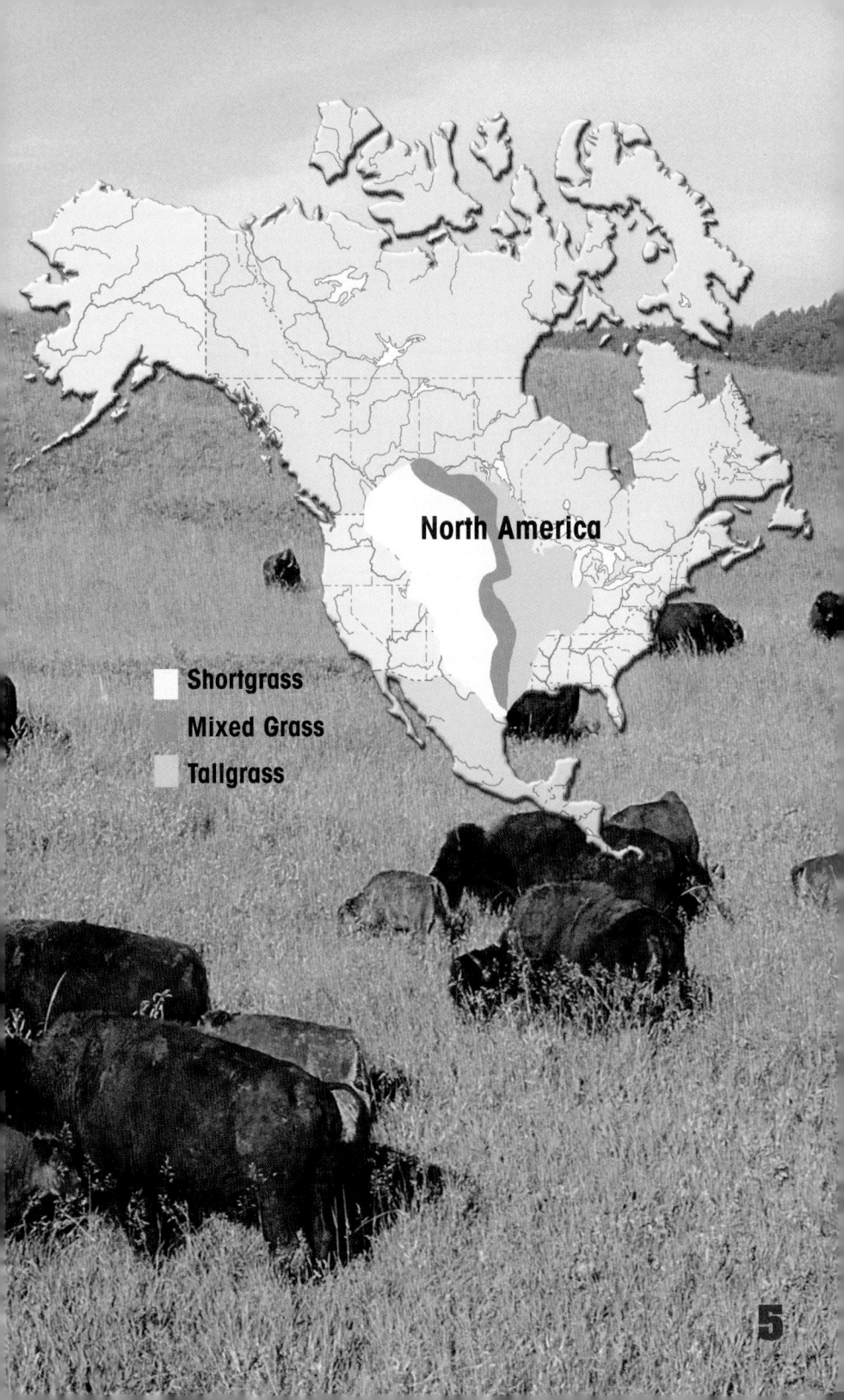

North America

Shortgrass

Mixed Grass

Tallgrass

Plants of the Prairie

Hundreds of different plants grow on the prairie. Some grasses, like big bluestem, can be nine or ten feet tall! Others, like buffalo grass, may be only four inches tall. Prairie flowers can also be short or tall. Black-eyed Susans may be only sixteen inches tall or as high as six feet tall. Sunflowers can be eight to ten feet tall!

The leaves, roots, and seeds of prairie plants provide food for many prairie animals. The taller grasses also help small animals hide from their enemies.

Native Americans used big bluestem to treat stomach problems. They used the roots of black-eyed Susans, the flowers shown here, to treat colds.

Fires and the Prairie

Prairies need fire as much as they need rain. Before many settlers lived on the prairie, fires were common. Lightning started many prairie fires.

Native Americans understood that the prairie needed fires. They often started prairie fires on purpose to help prairie plants grow.

Fires create the right growing conditions for prairie plants. They kill plants that don't belong on the prairie, like trees. The fires don't hurt the young leaves of native plants, which start growing below the ground. Once the plants that don't belong on the prairie are gone, the native plants get more sun and can grow better.

Buffalo

About 60 million buffalo once lived on the prairie. Buffalo are the largest land animals in North America. Males may be six feet tall and weigh 2,000 pounds! Females weigh about half that much. Buffalo can live to be twenty years old.

Like other **grazing** animals, buffalo eat grasses and flowering plants. They live in herds of four to twenty. When scared, a herd **stampedes**. The huge animals can run thirty miles an hour!

Native Americans living on the prairie honored the buffalo as the wisest and strongest of all animals. Most honored of all was the white buffalo.

Prairie Dogs

Prairie dogs are really squirrels. They are called "dogs" because they make a barking sound. They live in families of one male, one to four females, and their young. They make their homes in **burrows** under the ground. A group of burrows is called a town.

Each day, prairie dogs look for grass, seeds, and **insects** to eat. They take care of their burrows and visit each other. One prairie dog in each family watches for enemies and barks if they see one.

Prairie dogs greet each other by gently touching their front teeth together. This is how they recognize each other.

Other Prairie Mammals

Buffalo and prairie dogs are **mammals**. The prairie is home to many other mammals. Jackrabbits eat plants. Ground squirrels and mice eat plants, seeds, insects, and some small animals. Other mammals hunt the jackrabbits, squirrels, and mice for food.

Badgers use their strong front feet to dig squirrels and mice out of their burrows. Black-footed **ferrets** eat prairie dogs. Coyotes, foxes, and skunks hunt smaller prairie animals and also eat some plants.

Jackrabbits live in the shortgrass prairie, where it is easier to see their enemies. Ferrets and coyotes hunt animals that live in the shortgrass prairie.

Jackrabbit

Black-footed Ferret

Coyote

Birds of the Prairie

Prairie chickens live on the tallgrass prairie, where they hunt for insects to eat. Male prairie chickens put on quite a show to find mates. They spread out their feathers, puff up two orange pouches on their necks, and jump around, and dance.

Hawk

Prairie chickens and quail live on the tallgrass prairie, where they hide their nests in the grass. Hawks and cranes live on the shortgrass prairie.

Prairie Chicken

Quail

Crane

Two important prairie birds are meat eaters. The largest type of hawk in North America lives on the prairie and hunts prairie dogs and ground squirrels. Burrowing owls make their homes in empty prairie dog burrows and hunt small animals.

Reptiles and Amphibians

Prairie **reptiles** include snakes and lizards. Snakes eat birds and other small animals. The prairie skink, a striped lizard, eats insects and spends most of the day under rocks to stay cool.

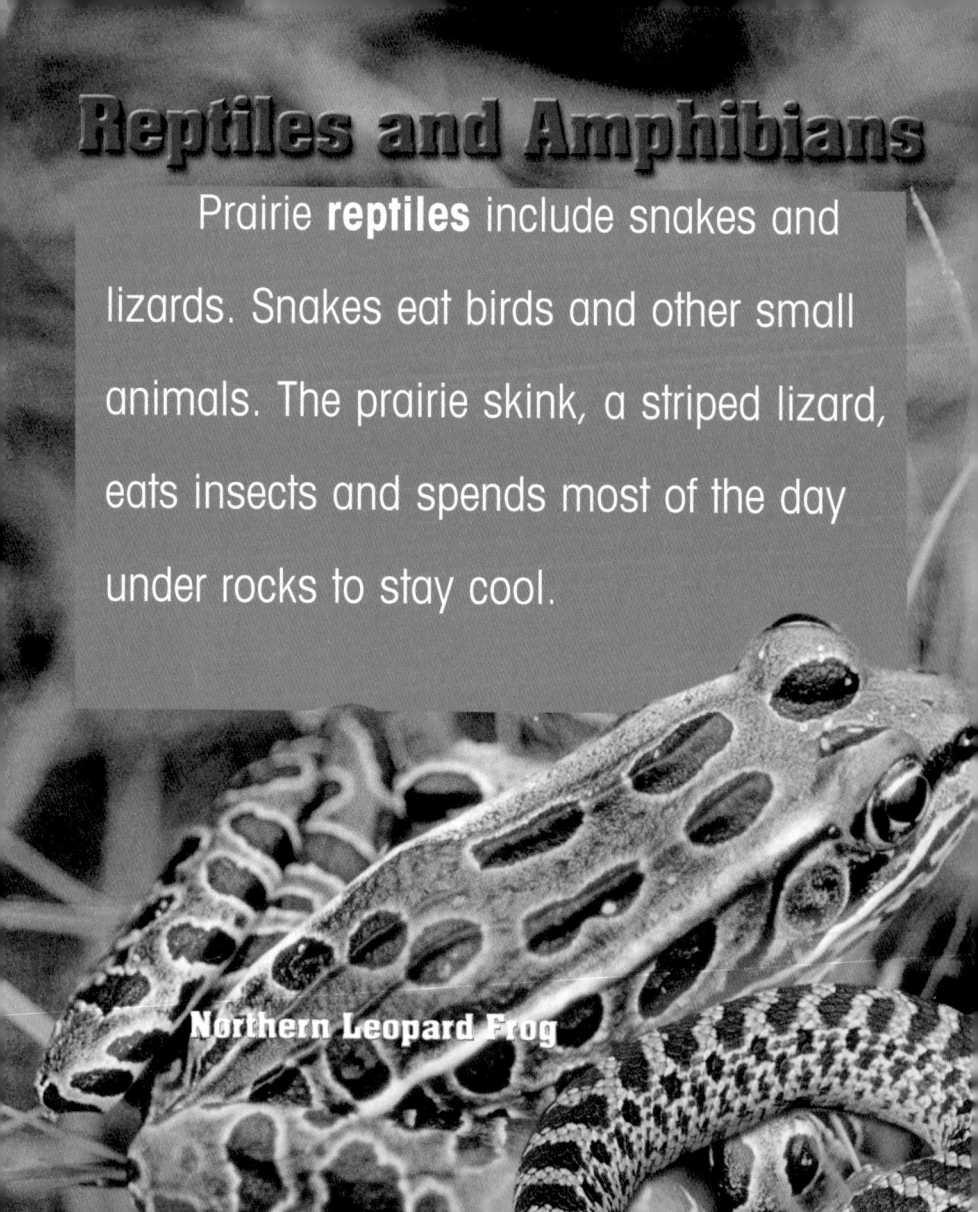

Northern Leopard Frog

Great Plains Toad

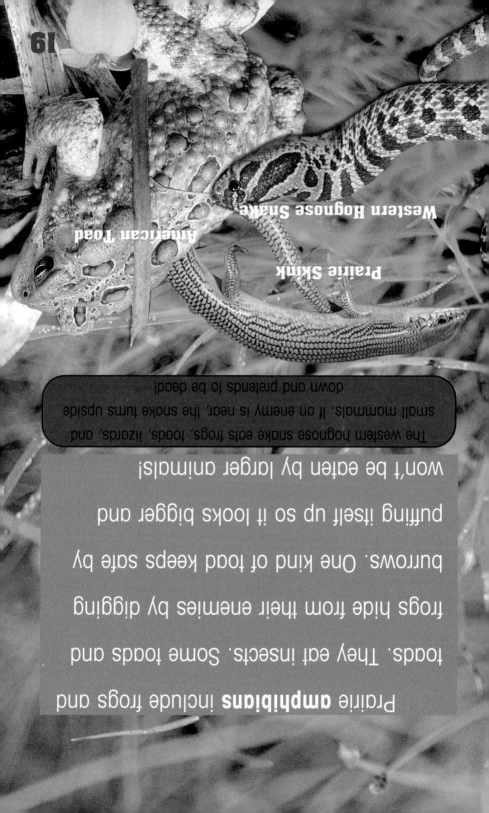

Western Hognose Snake

American Toad

Prairie Skink

Prairie **amphibians** include frogs and toads. They eat insects. Some toads and frogs hide from their enemies by digging burrows. One kind of toad keeps safe by puffing itself up so it looks bigger and won't be eaten by larger animals!

The western hognose snake eats frogs, toads, lizards, and small mammals. If an enemy is near, the snake turns upside down and pretends to be dead!

Insects of the Prairie

There are more insects on the prairie than any other kind of animal. Insects like grasshoppers, bees, and some beetles get their food from prairie plants. Ants and other beetles eat insects and dead animals.

One kind of ant raises insects called **aphids** (AY-fihdz) like people raise cows! They take care of the aphids and get a sweet liquid from them. The ants also eat some of the aphids.

The ants keep the aphids in rooms under the ground. They spend all of their time taking care of the aphids.

Saving the Prairie

The prairie is disappearing. Cities and farms have taken over most of the land. Only a few prairie chickens remain, because they can't live anywhere else. Farmers have killed most of the prairie dogs. Hunters have killed most of the buffalo.

Today, many people are working to save the prairie. They have created special areas where people can't build cities or farms. They keep prairie plants and animals safe so that we don't lose them forever.

Glossary

amphibian   An animal that lives in water when it is young and on land when it is grown. An amphibian is as warm or as cold as the air around it.

aphid   A tiny insect that drinks juices from plants.

burrow   A hole an animal digs in the ground for a place to live.

Fahrenheit   A measure of how hot or how cold something is.

ferret   A small, furry animal with a long body and short legs.

graze   To feed on grass and other plants that grow in fields and meadows.

insect   A small animal with three parts to its body and six legs. Bees, ants, and beetles are insects.

mammal   An animal that is often covered with hair or fur. Females give birth to live young and feed them milk from their bodies.

North America   A large mass of land between the Atlantic and Pacific Oceans. North America includes the United States, Canada, and Mexico.

reptile   An animal that is usually covered with scales, like a lizard. A reptile is as warm or as cold as the air around it.

stampede   To run in panic when scared.

temperature   How hot or cold something is.

Index